CONNECTIONS

Decisions

"God, I don't know what to do."

By Richard H. Wolkenhauer
Edited by Jane L. Fryar

CPH™
SAINT LOUIS

Editorial assistant: Marilyn T. Weber

This publication is available in braille and in large print for the visually impaired. Write to the Library for the Blind, 1333 South Kirkwood Road, St. Louis, MO 63122-7295. Allow six months for processing.

3558 South Jefferson Avenue, St. Louis, MO 63118-3968
Manufactured in the United States of America.

1 2 3 4 5 6 7 8 9 10 03 02 01 00 99 98 97 96 95 94

By mutual agreement . . .
and in the Holy Spirit's power

We will rely on the Holy Scriptures as our final authority,
knowing that human ideas and opinions,
even the ideas and opinions of God's people, will
likely stray from God's truth from time to time.

We will attend each session unless an
emergency prevents our attendance.

We will listen to each other and show one another
Christ-like love and concern.

We will contribute to the discussion in positive ways
as we are able to do that.

We will keep everything we hear confidential,
sharing it with no one unless doing so
is a matter (literally) of life and death.

We will use what we learn in this group to contribute
even more fully to the overall ministry of

____

(*Put your congregation's name here.*)

We will respect one another's schedules by
beginning and ending on time.

Contents

How to Use This Course

Three ingredients will make it possible for you to maximize the usefulness of this course. Let's look at these ingredients one at a time.

❖ 1—Prayer

Only as God invades our lives and touches our hearts can we grow up in Him. Ask and keep on asking for the Holy Spirit's direction and help as you approach His Word. Even if you work through the questions in this study on your own (and perhaps especially then), you must rely on God to do His work in you, His holy work of drawing you to Himself. He's the only one who can connect us to Himself and keep that connection strong. He's the only one who can connect us to our brothers and sisters in the faith and keep those connections strong. We need to ask Him to do that.

❖ 2—Care

That is, care for one another in your group. Dietrich Bonhoeffer once wrote, "Christianity means community through Jesus Christ and in Jesus Christ . . . we belong to one another only through and in Jesus Christ."

Only God can create the kind of care, the kind of community, the kind of connectedness that we see modeled by the early Christian church. It's His gift to His people. We can't make it happen, no matter how slick our techniques, no matter how smooth our approach.

But we can, by God's grace, encourage the kind of atmosphere, the kind of love and acceptance, in which His people come to know one another as brothers and sisters in the faith, and not as third or fourth cousins.

❖ 3—As We Share

How does that kind of love happen? We cannot drum it up by our own effort, no matter how up-to-date our methodology. Neither can we force any believer or group of believers to talk about their faith with one another, to share their needs and hurts with each other, or to admonish and console one another. We can, however, intentionally use what we know about human relationships to create a safe haven, an island of time and place, in which God's people can relax, get to know one another, and eventually feel free to let down their guard.

In this kind of setting, participants can experience the freedom to talk about their hurts and their faith with each other, if they choose to do that. They can encourage one another in the one true faith, just as the early Christians did and as the holy apostles also urge us to do as God's chosen people today (1 Thess. 4:18; 5:11).

❖ On to the Practical

As you develop small-group ministry in your congregation, you need to keep an overarching vision in mind. But to get small-group Bible study off the ground, and to keep it functioning effectively, you also need to think through some practical considerations.

Leadership

Talk with your pastor about this. He has both the right and the duty to oversee any Bible-study program in your congregation. He himself may lead some groups. And he may decide to delegate some leadership tasks, approving those who will teach and taking care to see that they receive adequate training.

In general, all those who lead small-group Bible studies will be people who

- demonstrate an understanding of Law and Gospel, sin and grace, not just intellectually, but in their relationships with God and with other people ;
- demonstrate an ability to communicate the truths of the Scriptures clearly;
- express a desire to be used by God to disciple others;
- show a commitment to the entire congregation and submission to the spiritual authority of the pastor, not competing with other leaders or programs;
- know or be willing to learn techniques that enable adults to examine and apply their faith to their daily lives;
- pray for the group and the congregation regularly;
- have time to plan, prepare, and lead a small-group Bible study on an ongoing, consistent basis;
- demonstrate the emotional and spiritual maturity to accept responsibilities of leadership, to receive direction and sometimes criticism with wisdom and grace, to share personal strengths and weaknesses with appropriate vulnerability, and to respond to others with Christ-like humility and love.

Setting

Many people find a home conducive to the relaxed, casual atmosphere you want to foster. In any case, you will need a meeting place where

- from 6–10 people can sit comfortably and see one another as they converse;
- the chairs are comfortable;
- the room is suitably lighted, ventilated, and at a comfortable temperature;

- coffee, tea, or soft drinks and an occasional snack can be served without danger of damaging carpets or upholstery;
- children can be adequately supervised while they play away from the Bible-study group.

Supplies

Everyone who attends should bring his or her own Bible. In addition you will need

- copies of this Study Guide for everyone (note the leaders materials in the back of this guide);
- pens or pencils, one for everyone;
- songbooks, hymnals, and perhaps an instrument to accompany singing during worship times;
- an empty chair or two placed prominently to remind everyone of the opportunity to invite guests—in particular, unchurched friends or relatives.

❖ That First Meeting

The first time you're together, you will want to spend some time getting to know one another and establishing rules for the group.

- Introduce yourselves to one another. Do this even if only one person is unfamiliar to the others. Tell your name. Tell a little about your family. And tell how you've come to be in the group. Use a timer and allow each person to speak for about a minute.
- Agree on ground rules about questions like these:
  Who will bring snacks? How often?
  Will we provide childcare? If so, how? Will we take turns, hire someone and agree to all chip in to pay for it? Or?
  Will we meet in one location? Take turns hosting the group? Or?
  When will we begin? End? (Include dates and also times.)
- Read "By Mutual Agreement" located on page 3 of this guide. Talk it over until everyone understands it and you truly have

reached mutual agreement. Promise to reread this agreement as you begin each session, at least the first several times you get together.

- Talk about participation. This study asks group members to work with partners or with three or four other people. Agree to listen to one another with respect. Also agree to allow one another the freedom to "pass" on any question for any reason without having to state that reason.
- Remind one another that everyone is entitled to an opinion. However, in this group all human opinions must take a back seat to the Holy Scriptures. You will share lots of thoughts and feelings with one another during the next few weeks. Even so, we believe that absolute truth exists and that it can be known because the God who created the universe has revealed the truth for us in His Word. We bow to His wisdom. We submit to His truth.

❖ Elements of Small-Group Bible Studies

Most groups spend 60–90 minutes together in these four activities:

- Worship
- Bible study
- Prayer
- Fellowship

Worship (5–15 minutes)

As most small-group Bible studies begin, participants spend a few minutes in worship. Often this includes singing, especially if someone in the group can play the guitar or piano. If the group does not include a musician, someone in the group can usually find an alternative that will allow everyone to join in singing two or three hymns or songs. Some groups find that they manage to sing quite well a cappella.

Some use prerecorded accompaniment tracks from cassette tapes or CDs.

Keep in mind, though, that worship involves much more than simply singing a few random songs. Worship should help participants quiet their hearts as the Lord prepares them to hear what He will say to them in His Word.

Therefore, opening worship will almost always include a prayer for His peace and for hearts ready to receive His truth.

Bible Study (40–60 minutes)

Our relationship with our Lord deepens as we immerse ourselves in His Word. In that Word He confronts us with our sin and then comforts us with His forgiving love in our Savior. Small-group Bible study at its best includes both of these elements.

Materials appropriate for small-group study avoid a lecture format. Rather, they involve a mix of individual thought and writing, one-on-one discussions, and give-and-take conversations by the whole group. The leader facilitates, asks questions, provides nuggets of insight to push the group's process forward, and prays for participants while they think and talk with one another.

Prayer—(5–10 minutes)

In the small-group Bible-study process, God's Word touches the hearts of His people. It probes pockets of hurt and sometimes of hardness. God's people talk with one another about life's most important issues. We think and laugh together. We question and cry together. It's only natural that we pray together too. It's not only natural, but necessary.

This kind of prayer models itself after that of the early church:

> They raised their voices together in prayer to God. . . . After they prayed, the place where they were meeting was shaken. And they were all filled with the Holy Spirit and spoke the word of God boldly. (Acts 4:24, 31)

Committed by God's grace to one another and to the truth of His Word, God's people asked their Lord to intervene in their lives. Together they asked for His specific help with specific challenges and needs. They united their hearts in praise to Him for all He had done and for all that He had promised yet to do. They received from Him the power they needed to live as His witnesses in a world that is, even now for the most part, hostile to the claims of Christ. We join them in the same kind of prayer.

Fellowship (10–20 minutes)

Christian fellowship means so much more than this spring's softball league or last Friday's fish fry. Of course, there is nothing wrong with playing softball or sharing a meal with other believers. But God intends that Christian fellowship (*koinonia*) cut more deeply below life's surface than that.

As we said earlier, only God can create genuine fellowship. It's His gift to His people. We can, however, provide unstructured time over coffee or lemonade before and after the more formal group time. This will free participants to laugh together, to cry together, to ask one another about ongoing personal and family concerns and simply to enjoy one another as members of God's family.

We witness spontaneously to one another about what God has done for us in Christ's cross and, then too, about what He is doing for us in our day-to-day lives. We have the chance to share specific prayer requests one-on-one and to become aware of needs God would use us to meet for each other. In short, we have a chance to be the church, the family of God, for one another.

❖ As You Begin This Course

Decisions, decisions! Life is full of decisions. Every day we must make choices. Some are easy. Others, because of their possible ramifications, are terribly difficult.

Sometimes we wish that our heavenly Father would come to us with specific guidance. If only He would take a megaphone and call out to us from heaven with answers.

But this is not the way it works. The one who has taken the initiative, who has chosen us by His grace and has made us His children, has gifted us with His Word and with the Sacraments. He has granted us the privilege of prayer.

He has given us relationships with other brothers and sisters in the faith—people who care about us and are willing to listen to us and to counsel us.

Blessed with these gifts, we can launch into the sea of decision-making. Ever living in His love, we can be sure that even when we make mistakes, even when we fear those mistakes may pull us down into the ocean's depths, He will be there for us. He will put His arms around us and whisper anew the comforting words He first spoke long ago, "Peace, be still!"

May your time together around God's Word help you grow in the grace that will enable you to face decisions with the confidence that has its source in His love.

Free to Choose 1

Setting Our Sights

Together we will see how sin has complicated our ability to make wise choices. We will see how our freedom in Christ impacts (or *can* impact) our decisions. Our goal will be to let God work through His Word to equip us to reach decisions that reflect our faith in Christ.

Getting Started

Take a few moments to become better acquainted with one other person in your group. If you feel comfortable about it, share a decision you made in the past week. Was there anything that made the decision difficult for you? If so, what? why?

Digging In

You've just touched upon some difficulties involved in making decisions. Now read aloud Romans 7:21–25 (on the next page).

So I find this law at work: When I want to do good, evil is right there with me. For in my inner being I delight in God's law; but I see another law at work in the members of my body, waging war against the law of my mind and making me a prisoner of the law of sin at work within my members. What a wretched man I am! Who will rescue me from this body of death? Thanks be to God—through Jesus Christ our Lord! (Romans 7:21–25)

1. Think about the words you have just read.

a. What is the basic problem the apostle Paul describes here?

b. In your earlier conversation about factors that complicate decision-making, did you talk about this problem? Why or why not?

2. On the one hand, Paul delights in a divine principle for good—theologians call this "the New Nature"—which is at work within him. Still he faces a disturbing principle, too—"the Old Nature."

a. To what historical biblical event can we trace Paul's "Old Nature" (and ours)?

b. What historical biblical event accounts for the "New Nature" that is at work in Paul's life?

3. Clearly the apostle finds himself very much frustrated by his quandary.

a. Does Paul's dilemma ring a bell with you? Explain.

b. Share (if you can do so comfortably) a situation from your own life that illustrates your kinship with Paul in this regard.

Jot some notes to yourself below. Then talk with a partner about the incident.

c. Which tends to shape most of your decisions, "God's Law" or the "law of sin"? Explain.

4. Reread the last two sentences of Romans 7:21–25 aloud and in unison. As complicated and frustrating as Paul's predicament is, it's not hopeless! Work together with your group to create a statement that tells how Jesus enables us to rise above our bondage to the "law of sin."

Hitting Home

Beth and Mark Jones, both Christians, are agonizing over a terrible problem. Beth's father was critically injured in an automobile accident a month ago. He has not regained consciousness and has been on a life support system since the day of the tragedy. Yesterday the doctors told Beth that there is no hope for her dad's recovery. They suggested that she authorize the removal of the life support and let him die. It would be all over, they estimated, within 24 to 48 hours.

Mark feels strongly that they ought to follow the doctors' advice. After all, there truly is no hope that Dad will regain consciousness, let alone get well.

Besides, his insurance coverage is limited. This means that Mark and Beth will likely have to get involved in paying for medical expenses. Mark says that this would not be fair to their four children, who would then be deprived because of it.

Beth doesn't think the decision is so obvious. After all, her father's life is at stake. She and her dad were very close, and he constantly made sacrifices for her through the years. Beth points out that doctors are only human and can make mistakes. Three years ago, Aunt Judy's physician gave her only six weeks to live—and she's still alive and enjoying life, too! Besides, God hears our prayers and performs miracles also in our day.

Beth and Mark both have compelling reasons to feel the way they do. But a decision must be made.

1. How could the "law of sin" affect their thinking?

2. How might the "law of God" apply here?

3. What do you think Beth and Mark should do? Why? Talk with your partner about your opinion and the reasons you feel as you do.

4. How would you explain the freedom we have in Christ to Beth and Mark in a way that might help them with their decision-making process.

5. Share, if you feel comfortable about it, a difficult decision you have had to make in the past or one you face now. What light has this lesson shined on that decision? Share, if you can do so comfortably, with your group.

Wrapping Up

Spend a few moments in silence, reflecting on personal decisions you have recently made—or failed to make. In 1 Corinthians 10:31 Paul writes: "So whether you eat or drink or whatever you do, do it all for the glory of God."

How might this passage apply to our decision-making?

The Extra Mile

Review—Abraham was able to make some tough decisions because of the faith that God gave him. Read about this in Galatians 3:6–14.

Preview—study 1 Peter 2:18–25. In verse 21, the Greek word for “example” means literally “tracing over” Christ. If He is indeed the example for our decision-making, would you think the priority in our decisions lies in being “correct” or in loving and serving?

Is there always a difference? Explain.

Motivated by Grace to Trace

2

Setting Our Sights

In this lesson we will discuss "tracing over" Christ as we make our decisions in the security of His grace. We want to look at our beautiful Savior and see anew how His redeeming love motivates us to want to "trace over" that love as we live out our lives as His people. We shall see how this relates to our decision-making.

Getting Started

Picture a child working with tracing paper and a pencil. She wants to reproduce a drawing of a tiger from the page beneath the tracing paper. With painstaking care she outlines the big cat's body and then goes on to fill in the details of the picture. At long last her work is completed. With excitement she rushes into the kitchen to show her mother what she has done.

Mom notices the likeness of the tiger. But right away she also sees how imperfectly her young daughter has done her work. The lines are not always true. There are gaps and mistakes. But the mother takes the child into her arms and hugs her, happy at heart for her little girl and thankful God has given her a precious daughter.

In 1 Peter 2:21 we are told that Christ left an example for us "that [we] should follow in

His steps." The Greek word "example" carries the idea of "tracing over" Christ. We who have been adopted as God's children because of His grace in Christ Jesus, are called to imitate Jesus, to replicate His life in ours.

Like the little girl, we don't always do such a great job in "tracing over" Christ. We make errors. Our lines are often ragged. In fact, sometimes we just plain make a mess of it. But the Lord, looking at our imperfect tracing job, nevertheless opens His arms wide to us in love, rejoicing in us as His sons and daughters. Our good works, our ability to make perfect decisions have nothing to do with our position. That depends only on His grace. But that very grace motivates us to want to "trace over" Christ.

1. What human being have you most wanted to be like? Why?

2. If you could flip a switch and become totally like Christ in one trait, what characteristic would you choose? Explain.

Digging In

As you study Matthew 4:1–11, ask yourself how you would rate Jesus as a decision-maker. How did He make His decisions? Why?

Then Jesus was led by the Spirit into the desert to be tempted by the devil. After fasting forty days and forty nights, He was hungry. The tempter came to him and said, "If you are the Son of God, tell these stones to become bread."

Jesus answered, "It is written: 'Man does not live on bread alone, but on every word that comes from the mouth of God.' "

Then the devil took Him to the holy city and had Him stand on the highest point of the temple. "If you are the Son of God," he said, "throw yourself down. For it is written: 'He will command His angels concerning you; and they will lift you up in their hands, so that you will not strike your foot against a stone.' "

Jesus answered him: "It is also written: 'Do not put the Lord your God to the test.' "

Again, the devil took Him to a very high mountain and showed Him all the kingdoms of the world and their splendor. "All this I will give You," he said, "if You will bow down and worship me."

Jesus said to him, "Away from Me, Satan! For it is written: 'Worship the Lord God, and serve Him only.' "

Then the devil left Him, and angels came and attended Him. (Matthew 4:1–11)

1. Did you notice that these temptations of Jesus are much like those that we face? Did you also see that in confronting each temptation Jesus used a passage from Scripture?

a. Think back on decisions you've made in the past. Have you always based them on this same criterion—the Word of God? Tell about a time you, by God's grace, did that.

b. What decision(s) have you made that, in retrospect, you wish you had used this criterion? Share one of these with a partner, if you can do so comfortably.

c. The account of Jesus' temptation illustrates what theologians have called Christ's "active obedience." By this they mean that Jesus obeyed God's Law in our place. What comfort does this give you as you think about decisions you regret having made?

2. Jesus based all of His decisions squarely on the Father's Word and will.

a. Why is knowing Scripture so important for us as we face tough decisions?

b. Give some examples of dilemmas that are not specifically addressed in the Bible.

c. If we fail to find Bible passages that apply to particular choices that we must make, can we nonetheless make use of God's Word in our decision-making? Explain.

3. Look back at Matthew 4:1–11. As our Savior made His choices, some specific attitudes guided Him. Which words imply that

Jesus loved His Father and wanted to honor Him?

Jesus had come to carry out His Father's will?

Jesus loved us with an uncompromising love?

In fact, in love He would later lay down His life for us.

Hitting Home

Keeping in mind everything we've looked at so far in this session, tear into a decision you are confronting right now. Apply the principles that we have been discussing.

1. What Bible passages or biblical concepts apply to this situation?

2. What course of action would most clearly reflect your love for God and His priorities for your life? Explain.

3. What response would best demonstrate a "tracing over" Him who prayed to His Father, "May Your will be done"?

4. What course of action would "trace over" Jesus, who evidenced such an amazing love for others, even sacrificing His own life for them? Explain.

Wrapping Up

Spend a few moments citing examples of Christ-like decision-making that you have observed in the Christian community. Thank God for the good decisions He empowers those in authority to make.

The Extra Mile

Review—browse through Hebrews 11:1–40 and note what was Christ-like about the decisions of your spiritual ancestors mentioned there.

Preview—go through Hebrews 11:1–40 again. As you read, watch for what motivated and empowered these ancestors of all the faithful.

3 Empowered by Grace to Choose

Setting Our Sights

The apostle Paul calls the Gospel "the power of God" (Romans 1:16). From the Greek word for "power" comes our English word *dynamite.* The Gospel of Jesus Christ is God's dynamite! Today we will look at ways God empowers us through Word and Sacrament to make the best of our decisions.

Getting Started

Some decisions torment us. Usually they involve, not choosing between good and bad, right and wrong, but between something good and something better or between better and best. How do we decide?

We may well find ourselves wishing that God would use a skywriter to let us know what the best course of action would be. With a partner or in your whole group, tell about a time you agonized over a decision like this—between good and better, between better and best. Share, not just the facts of the situation, but also your struggle at the time as best as you can remember it.

Digging In

Last time, we talked about "tracing over" Christ, about how we live out our lives to His glory in response to His saving love. But Christ is far more than simply our model for effective decision-making.

Study Ephesians 2:1–10. See if you can discover how, by grace, Jesus empowers us to do what is good and right.

As for you, you were dead in your transgressions and sins, in which you used to live when you followed the ways of this world and of the ruler of the kingdom of the air, the spirit who is now at work in those who are disobedient.

All of us also lived among them at one time, gratifying the cravings of our sinful nature and following its desires and thoughts. Like the rest, we were by nature objects of wrath.

But because of His great love for us, God, who is rich in mercy, made us alive with Christ even when we were dead in transgressions—it is by grace you have been saved.

And God raised us up with Christ and seated us with Him in the heavenly realms in Christ Jesus, in order that in the coming ages He might show the incomparable riches of His grace, expressed in His kindness to us in Christ Jesus.

For it is by grace you have been saved, through faith—and this not from yourselves, it is the gift of God—not by works, so that no one can boast.

For we are God's workmanship, created in Christ Jesus to do good works, which God prepared in advance for us to do. (Ephesians 2:1–10)

1. Underline the words in which the apostle makes its crystal clear that we are incapable of choosing Christ to be our Savior.

2. Who, then, takes the initiative in saving us? Put a wavy line under the words that emphasize this.

3. Paul refers to "grace" three times in these 10 verses. Write out a definition of "grace."

4. In 2 Corinthians 5:15 the apostle Paul writes: "And [Christ] died for all, that those who live should no longer live for themselves, but for Him who died for them and rose again." What verses in Ephesians 2:1–10 really say the same thing? Write those words here.

5. Look again at these words: "But because of His great love for us, God, who is rich in mercy, made us alive with Christ . . ."

a. What do you think it means to be "alive with Christ"?

b. It has been said that "what we do grows out of who we are." How does who we are in Christ affect what we do with our lives?

c. How does it affect (or how could it affect) the tough decisions you have made in the past or you are making now?

d. What growth might not take place if God hired skywriters to dictate the details of our decisions?

Hitting Home

Rose has just learned that she is pregnant. She is devastated by this news. She is not married. Her career has just gotten off the ground. The father of the baby is a nice person, but Rose isn't sure that she loves him enough to marry him.

Rose's friends laugh at her because she feels guilty about having had sex outside of marriage. They also think she's foolish for not considering an abortion. But Rose knows that the Holy Scriptures forbid both premarital sex and abortion. Still, her beliefs seem to have her trapped in a nearly impossible position. Think about Rose's predicament in light of her Christian faith.

1. How could Rose's relationship with Christ help her with her guilt? What could Rose do if feelings of guilt continue to trouble her?

2. What decisions does Rose face? What factors does Rose need to keep in mind as she makes these decisions?

3. If you were to face a decision of a magnitude similar to the one Rose faces, in what areas would you need Christ's empowerment? (Check as many as apply.)

___ In being assured of God's forgiveness
___ In guidance as to what to do
___ In facing the embarrassment caused by your sin
___ In finding the strength to avoid similar mistakes in the future

4. We all face difficult decisions now and then. Complete this sentence: *When it's really tough to decide an issue, then*

Wrapping Up

Sometimes in life we make "good" decisions—but for one reason or another the results aren't what we had hoped. On the other hand, sometimes we make "bad" decisions, but, as we struggle with them and pray over them, God brings good out of them anyway.

1. Give an example of a "good" decision that did not work out well in your life.

2. Give an example of a "bad" decision that was transformed by God's grace and became a blessing to you.

3. What does this tell you about future difficult decisions?

The Extra Mile

Review—prayerfully read Psalm 46. Take some quiet moments to reflect on God's promise to empower His people.

Preview—carefully read Acts 2:42–47. Consider how your being part of God's Christian community might enhance your ability to make wise choices.

Enabled by Grace to Help 4

Setting Our Sights

Are you comfortable in sharing your dilemmas and your problems with your brothers and sisters in Christ? Are the choices you make the church's business? Can our Christian fellowship be a blessing when it comes to making decisions?

In this lesson we will consider how we benefit from our involvement with others in Christ's church when we make decisions and carry them out. We will also see our role in our congregation as it relates to helping others make and live out their decisions.

Getting Started

Karen Clancy's husband walked out on her four years ago, leaving her to care for their three young children. Karen hasn't heard from her husband all this time. She works as a secretary in a small office, earning barely enough money to pay for life's necessities.

Some time ago her doctor advised Karen that she should undergo surgery. At the present time the surgery is in the elective category, but Karen has been warned that it would not be at all wise to put it off for too long.

Karen feels that it's important to have the surgery soon. But making the decision as to the timing of the operation is difficult. Who will take care of the children? Her relatives all live out of state. Besides, she doesn't have enough sick leave accumulated. She would earn no money at all for at least two weeks while she recuperates. Who will care for her when she gets home from the hospital? It's absolutely hopeless, Karen believes. Her decision is further complicated by the fact that she serves as the nursery attendant at her church, and there never seems to be anyone willing to assist her.

Suppose that you are a member of Karen's congregation. You have heard about her plight. Talk with a partner about these questions:

1. What could you do to help Karen make a good decision and implement that decision?

2. What could the congregation do to make the decision easier for Karen?

3. Sometimes it happens that the church actually makes some decisions more difficult. Share some thoughts on how this could happen in Karen's case.

Digging In

In Colossians 3:12–17, the apostle Paul describes a supportive fellowship. Read the words of this passage thoughtfully.

> Therefore, as God's chosen people, holy and dearly loved, clothe yourselves with compassion, kindness, humility, gentleness and patience. Bear with each other and forgive whatever grievances you may have against one another. Forgive as the Lord forgave you. And over all these virtues put on love, which binds them all together in perfect unity.
>
> Let the peace of Christ rule in your hearts, since as members of one body you were called to peace. And be thankful. Let the word of Christ dwell in you richly as you teach and admonish one another with all wisdom, and as you sing psalms, hymns and spiritual songs with gratitude in your hearts to God. And whatever you do, whether in word or deed, do it all in the name of the Lord Jesus, giving thanks to God the Father through Him. (Colossians 3:12–17)

Notice that Paul is writing to "God's chosen people." He is addressing these Spirit inspired words to those who believe in the Lord Jesus Christ, those who have tasted His magnificent forgiving love. The apostle is talking about how we respond to Jesus' grace.

1. Do you live in the security that you are "holy and dearly loved" in Christ? Explain.

2. How can this realization help you when you are called upon to make tough decisions?

3. What is the practical significance of knowing that we are "members of one body"?

4. What practical implication does this have for the decisions you are facing right now?

5. How can decisions made by individual Christians have an effect, either positive or negative, on the entire congregation. Give an example of this.

6. We notice that Paul mentions a number of virtues in this section of Scripture. Underline them in the text. How might these virtues be implemented by members of the congregation in Karen's situation?

- Compassion—

- Kindness—

- Humility—

- Gentleness—

- Patience—

7. This text reminds us that love binds all these virtues together. The Greek word that Paul uses here for love is *agape,* which might be described as "selfless devotion."

a. Christ's love is "agape." Mention as many ways as you can that He manifested this selfless devotion.

b. How could the exercise of this kind of love on the part of a congregation make decision-making by individual members easier?

c. When have you seen this happen in your congregation? Give several specific examples.

d. When is the exercise of this kind of love most likely to break down in your congregation? Why do you think this is?

Hitting Home

1. What could you do to help make sure that all members of your congregation would feel free to share their dilemmas with other believers in the congregation?

2. Would you be comfortable about such sharing with others in your congregation when you face a difficult decision? What could you do now to build bridges so that you would feel more comfortable asking for help when you need it?

Wrapping Up

Turn to Psalm 133. Read these words slowly, each member of the class following along in his or her own Bible.

The Extra Mile

In your devotions this week, treat yourself to Romans 12:1–21. Reflect on what you have learned and shared in this class as you do that.

In Conclusion

God does help us in our decision-making. He shares with us His Word and His Sacraments to strengthen and empower us. He places us in our church family, so that we do not stand alone when we come to the crossroads of life.

As we make decisions, we want—above all else—to bring honor to our Lord and Savior. Sometimes, by His grace, we'll do just that. On other occasions, we will make a terrible mess of things.

Still, He is always with us, ready to forgive us who have been drawn to Him who gave His life for us on the cross. His grace is ever-sufficient. His strength is made perfect in our weakness. The Lord will lift us up when we fall. He can even turn a bad decision into one that brings good into our lives.

We can trust our heavenly Father every step of life's way. Being sure of this, may we boldly face our decision-making moments, confident in His amazing grace!

Helps for the Leader

1—Free to Choose

Getting Started

(*10–12 minutes.*) Welcome the participants warmly. If this is the first experience some of them have had with small group Bible study, you may want to spend some time going over "How to Use This Course." Focus attention as well on "By Mutual Agreement" (p. 3 of this guide). Even if your group has completed several other studies from the Connections series, you will want to review this agreement.

Then ask everyone to turn to the last section of the introductory material, "As You Begin This Course." Read it to the group. Stress that, as much as we at times might wish otherwise, God has chosen to communicate with us through the means of grace—His Word and the Sacraments. He wants very much to help us in our decision-making, but He does not shout out guidance from the heavens or hire skywriters directing us to move to Chicago or to buy the house on 45th Street. We use the tools He's given us, and we stay close to our Lord as we meditate on His Word. The better we know our Savior, the more our decisions will reflect His wisdom and His priorities for our lives.

It is also important to emphasize that we do not and cannot make decisions about the most critical life-issue. Jesus Himself has told us: "You did not choose me, but I chose you" (John 15:16). The Holy Spirit leads us to faith in Christ. As we follow our Savior, we respond to His magnificent grace, seeking to make those decisions that will honor Him who first loved us.

Don't belabor these points. Simply mention them, returning to the principles later when the issues surface again—as they almost certainly will.

Read "Setting Our Sights," which charts your path for this first lesson. Then move into the "Getting Started" activity. Use this time to help class members get to know one another. You might use an ice breaker of some kind. Perhaps you could ask a few questions such as these:

- Who was born farthest away from here?
- Who thinks he or she has the most unusual hobby?
- What was the best job you ever had?

Then ask class members who feel comfortable in so doing to share with one other person a decision they made in the past week. Tell them you are not asking anyone to talk about a traumatic decision, but simply any decision—no matter how trivial—that comes to mind. Encourage them to discuss briefly anything that may have made the decision difficult and why this factor complicated it.

Digging In

(*18 minutes.*) Have someone in the class read the text printed in the lesson (Rom. 7:21–25). Then work through the questions that follow.

1. (a) Paul finds himself in a battle, and he's not only at war with himself, he's also the battlefield! He delights in God's Law, but there is another law, "the law of sin," he calls it, that makes him a prisoner.

b. Let the class comment on this.

2. (a) The fall into sin is responsible. All of us have inherited Adam's sinful nature.

b. Because Jesus suffered, died, and rose again to pay for our sins, God can give fallen human beings new life through faith in what the Savior has done. This "new nature" comes to us as God's gift, not because of anything we have done to earn or deserve it. As time will allow, refer participants to Rom. 6:1–6 and 2 Cor. 5:17–21.

3. (a) No doubt everyone will be able to identify with Paul in his dilemma. Ask for comments and specific evidence as time will allow.

b. Encourage partners to keep this sharing light, so that no one feels threatened by it. You should probably share an example from your own life first to help break the ice.

c. Answers will vary. Perhaps participants would feel more comfortable sharing with a partner rather than with the whole group. Or let everyone think about this and jot down some notes for their own eyes only. In any case, encourage some "self-examination" here.

4. The previous questions, no doubt, will lead participants to see their sin, their failures to obey God's Law. This question applies the Good News of God's forgiveness to our hearts. It affords the group an opportunity to think through this matter creatively.

A sample statement might include some of the following thoughts: Jesus died on the cross to free us from the shackles of sin. In Christ, we have been placed into a beautiful relationship with our heavenly Father. We have become part of His family, fully forgiven in Christ, free to manifest His love. We can make our decisions within the framework of His grace, knowing that even when we make bad choices, He still loves us, we can still call ourselves His children, and we can still rejoice that we have been forgiven through the precious blood of Jesus.

Hitting Home

(*12 minutes.*) Ask volunteers to share in reading a portion of the dilemma Beth and Mark Johnson face. You might want to ask the class to form groups of four. Discuss, either in small groups or all together, the questions that follow the story.

1. Answers will vary. For example, Beth and Mark might be tempted to consider the question selfishly. What decision would be personally easiest for them? How could they avoid major expenditure of family funds? Or what would evoke the least emotional burden?

2. Again, answers will vary. As Beth and Mark respond to God's redeeming love for them, the "law of God" can take over. They can consider one another's needs, Dad's needs, and the love that God's Law commands them to show.

3. Various ideas will probably be forthcoming. Try to get the class members to share the rationale they used in coming to their conclusions.

4. Surely a Christian will not want to act contrary to anything that God makes clear in His Word. The love of Christ constrains us to desire to honor Him. His love for us frees us from our selfishness to consider how we might best demonstrate His love in any decision we face—no matter how complex. And His love frees us from the paralysis of thinking we must make perfect decisions, only and always.

Because we live in a fallen world and because the "Old Nature" will cling to us until we go home to live with Jesus forever, our decisions will often carry the taint of selfishness. Then, too, we're not omniscient. Our insight is limited.

Relying on Christ's love, we make the tough decisions we must make. And even as we do that, we trust that it is not the correctness of our decisions that keeps us right with God, but always and only His grace. On that we can rely.

5. By this time, the members of the class may feel more comfortable sharing significant situations and feelings. Give them time to talk about this question with a partner or with the whole group.

Wrapping Up

(*3 minutes.*) Encourage individuals prayerfully to consider 1 Cor. 10:31 and how it relates to any decisions they face now. It would be appropriate, after a couple of minutes have elapsed, to close with a prayer, inviting those who would like to do so to add a brief petition of their own.

The Extra Mile

(*2 minutes.*) Point out two parts in this section—review and preview. Encourage class members to look this section over and involve themselves in the questions as they have time and opportunity in the days ahead. Ask them especially to think about the "tracing over" idea set forth in the preview section. This will prepare them for the material to be presented next time.

2—Motivated by Grace to Trace

Getting Started

(*10 minutes.*) Have the class take a quick look at "Setting Our Sights" to see what you want to accomplish together today.

Then read aloud the account of the child working with tracing paper. Ask group members to respond to the questions. If your group did well working with partners last time, suggest that they pair off now and talk about the questions with their partner. (Note that most times it's best if people work with someone other than their spouse or best friend.)

1. Any person might be cited—a family member, a friend, some celebrity. The value of this question lies in the answer to why and in the process of exploring that answer.

2. In order to get the conversation started, you might give an example or two of Christ's traits: humility, patience, self-sacrificing love, and so on.

Digging In

(*15 minutes.*) You could begin this section by mentioning that Jesus, like us, regularly confronted decisions. Today's Scripture reading presents three crucial choices that our Savior was called upon to make. Have volunteers read Matt. 4:1–11 aloud.

1. (a) Invite participants to share, perhaps with a partner. It may help group members think of examples from their lives if you first give one from your own.

b. This question will be harder—more threatening—for most people. Acknowledge this and, once again, share an example from your own life. Then invite partners to talk about it. Encourage them to choose an example they can share comfortably. Remind them, too, of the "pass option."

c. Jesus kept God's Law perfectly in our place. He—unlike we ourselves—always made perfect decisions. Then He died on the cross in our place to take the punishment we deserved for our sinful decisions as well as for all our other sins (passive obedience). Now, God credits Jesus' righteousness (His "rightness," His perfect obedience) to our account. How comforting to be able to rely on this at times when we know we've failed to "trace over" Christ's holiness!

2. (a) Scripture reveals God's will and God's ways to us. Because God has loved us so dearly through Jesus, who died for us and rose again, we want to live out our lives in a manner that will reflect His glorious love. "We love because He first loved us" (1 John 4:19).

b. The key word here is "specifically." Let volunteers give examples. For instance, the dilemma Beth and Mark faced in the last session has no specific biblical resolution. The Bible does not tell us who, specifically, to marry or where, specifically, to live. It does not prescribe the kind of car we are to drive or tell us whether we should rely on public transportation instead of owning our own car. Accept responses individuals can justify.

c. Absolutely! God's love is there to motivate and strengthen us. He shares wonderful wisdom and sets forth helpful principles in the Bible. Our goal in looking at Scripture, in most cases when we face a decision, is to find not "proof texts," but rather to remind ourselves of Christ's character and of our Father's promise to conform us "to the likeness of His Son" (Rom. 8:29). Then, confident in His forgiving love, we can consider our options in the light of God's glory and of our own and our neighbor's welfare.

3. Answers will vary. Accept reasonable responses: vv. 4, 7, and 10 all imply that Jesus loved the Father and that He had come to carry out the Father's will. The fact that Jesus subjected Himself to physical deprivation and temptation and submitted to the Law of God in our place points powerfully to His uncompromising love for us.

Hitting Home

(*About 15 minutes.*) Encourage participants as a group to choose a decision of some significance if possible, but even one of minor consequence will do.

Work through the questions together, one by one, as these apply to the sample decision.

Then ask group members to think of a personal decision they face. Have them work in pairs or, if it is more comfortable, individually to answer the questions again, this time as those questions apply to their personal decisions.

The answers to the questions will, of course, vary according to the decision under consideration.

Wrapping Up

(*5 minutes.*) Focus on decisions made in the context of the local congregation or of the church-at-large. Then spend some moments in prayer, either silently or aloud, thanking God for the good decisions He empowers those in authority to make.

The Extra Mile

Quickly refer to the review and preview assignments. Encourage participants to complete these before you convene next time.

3—Empowered by Grace to Choose

Getting Started

(*10 minutes.*) As you begin, point out that this session includes a lot of material. Ask that everyone make a conscious effort to keep the discussion moving.

Then read "Setting Our Sights" to the group and have a volunteer read the paragraphs that will set up today's discussion ("Getting Started").

After partners have time to share, spend a few moments discussing ungodly methods to which people sometimes turn for help in making decisions. Ask the class to suggest some of these (e.g., astrology, palm reading, Ouija boards.) Be sure to make it clear that the approaches just mentioned are anti-Scriptural and not God pleasing.

Ask class members if they think it might be helpful if God were to blare out specific answers or advice from heaven or send out advice on a divine fax machine. After volunteers have commented, continue by asking whether or not earthly parents do their children a favor if they always intervene in their children's decisions, if they always direct or override their children's choices.

Digging In

(*20 minutes.*) In this section we seek to make it clear that Christ is much more than just a model whom we seek to emulate. He is not merely an example of lofty morality. He is not simply someone over whom we "trace" our lives. Make it crystal clear that Jesus empowers us by His grace to decide to do what is good and right as He works through His Word and the Sacraments.

Have volunteers take turns reading the paragraphs in the Scripture passage. Then move on to the questions that follow.

1. Such references include the following:

- "You were dead in your transgressions and sins."
- "Gratifying the cravings of our sinful nature and following its desires and thoughts."
- "Like the rest, we were by nature objects of wrath."

2. God takes the initiative. Participants may underline passages such as these:

- "Because of His great love for us, God, who is rich in mercy, made us alive with Christ."
- "It is the gift of God."
- "We are God's workmanship."

3. A sample definition of grace: undeserved love.

4. "For we are God's workmanship, created in Christ Jesus to do good works . . ."

5. (a) It means to walk in the joyful knowledge that by God's grace we have been rescued from the eternal death we deserved because of our sin and have been brought into a saving relationship with God in which we enjoy abundant and eternal life by His grace through faith in Christ Jesus.

b. Various responses are possible. Stress that our being alive in Christ assures us of forgiveness and relieves us of the stress of having to do right and be right in order to receive God's favor. Being alive in Christ also assures us of His strength as we make decisions. Having become Christ's people and living in awareness of His love for us changes our thoughts, desires, words, and deeds. We want, more and more, to be like Him.

c. Responses will vary. Accept reasonable comments.

d. Encourage some discussion here.

Hitting Home

(*10 minutes.*) As you lead the class through this section, be sure to avoid a debate about abortion. Scripture settles this issue for us by speaking out clearly about the sacredness of human life. Rose knows this. Focus instead on the questions of how Rose can make decisions about her current situation that will best serve to glorify God, benefit her baby, and enable her to become more like Christ.

1. Crushed by the Law, Rose can be encouraged by the Gospel. There is forgiveness at the cross. Check Rom. 8:1ff. If Rose continues to be troubled by feelings of guilt, she may want to speak to her pastor or to another believer about it. The Scriptures have much to say about the comfort God gives as His people assure one another of His forgiveness and as we receive absolution from Christ through our pastor (cf. James 5:16; Matt. 18:15–18; John 20:22–23).

2. Encourage the class to discuss this frankly. They may mention financial needs, the baby's future welfare, Rose's own hopes for her life, and other, similar concerns. Stress most of all God's concern that Rose receives His love and forgiveness and that she demonstrate a Christ-like attitude in whatever actions she decides to take.

Life for Rose will not be easy in the coming months, but the Lord Jesus will use His Word to reassure and strengthen her if she will let Him do that. This assurance is not merely a pious platitude. It really works in individual lives as God fulfills His promise to work in everything for the good of His people (Rom. 8:28).

3. This question lends itself to personal thought. Most participants will likely check all four statements.

4. Have class members volunteer to complete the sentence. Responses should mention the benefits of personally studying God's Word, the counsel of Christian friends, submission to God, prayer, and the patience and willingness to wait for what our Lord wants to give His people.

Wrapping Up

(*5 minutes.*) Have group members who feel comfortable quickly share from their own experience examples that illustrate the two possibilities mentioned. Then ask individuals to comment on item 3.

The Extra Mile

Direct students to these voluntary assignments. They are self-explanatory.

4—Enabled by Grace to Help

Getting Started

(*10 minutes.*) Have a volunteer read "Setting Our Sights." Note that the questions in this section are not intended for discussion at this point. They are meant to stimulate thought.

Have a second volunteer read Karen Clancy's story. Ask the group to think about it for a few moments, imagining that they are all members of Karen's congregation. Discuss the questions that follow.

1. Answers will vary. Some might provide care for Karen's children, offer to do housework, take over the church nursery for the interim, bring meals to Karen, and so on.

2. Answers will vary. The congregation might offer financial help. The pastor could offer to counsel with her. Accept reasonable responses.

3. Ask for thoughts as to how Karen's congregation might make Karen's decision more difficult. For example, the leadership could make Karen feel guilty about the nursery situation and suggest that she postpone her surgery until someone volunteers to take over her duties. Members might inundate Karen with platitudes, e.g., "I'd like to help out, but it's just not a good time for me. But don't worry, God will work things out." As time will allow, refer participants to James 2:15ff.

Digging In

(*20 minutes.*) Have someone read the words from Colossians 3. Stress that Paul is addressing these words to believers. He is talking about our response to God's grace in Jesus Christ.

1. Some have grown up seeing God as a frowning judge who is out to get us. It is important for us to know and trust that we are dearly loved. Encourage participants to discuss this question with a partner.

2. God does not put us on trial when we make decisions. He will not punish us if we don't "get it right." God loves us! He sent His Son to die for us! He is on our side! He wants to help us. Stress again our freedom in Christ and the security we enjoy in His forgiving love.

3. We have brothers and sisters in the Lord who care about us and will stand beside us.

4. Answers will vary.

5. Ask participants to work with a partner to prepare a list of examples. Then ask each pair of participants to share their list. Since the church of Jesus Christ truly is one body, the actions of individual members do affect the whole—for good or ill. Decisions that weaken us spiritually will compromise our witness to the community and our service to our brothers and sisters in the faith, and vice versa.

6. Answers will vary. Accept reasonable responses.

7. (a) Jesus left the glories of heaven to live in the "slums" of a sin-filled earth. He took on Himself the form of a servant. He died for us upon the cross. Accept other specific ideas from the group. As time will permit refer the group to Phil. 2:5–8. Jesus did all this even though we had made ourselves His enemies. Even though there was no worthiness in us, He loved us!

b. Love like this does not set up qualifications. It demands no "admission fee." Our worth to one another (just like our worth to God) is not based on the correctness of our choices. Relaxing in that love, we can think and pray with less pressure, less tension, and are probably able to make wiser choices. Also, as with Karen Clancy, we will often be able to choose more wisely if we have others to support our decisions by providing practical help.

c and ***d.*** Invite an honest exchange of thoughts.

Hitting Home

(*10 minutes.*) This section contains questions that could be a bit touchy. Encourage class members to share in a spirit of love; not of judgment. We are not out to be critical, but to build up and help. Encourage the group to focus on what they—as individuals—could do to change things that need changing.

Wrapping Up

(*5 minutes.*) Read Psalm 133 as suggested. Then you might want to read to the class the paragraphs found in "In Conclusion." If time permits, spend a few moments in evaluating what you have learned.

The Extra Mile

Refer this assignment to participants for their private study.

In Conclusion

Have a volunteer read this summary aloud. Thank group members for their participation and wish them God's blessings in their future decision making.